IMPERMANENT WAYS

THE CLOSED LINES OF BRITAIN   -   VOLUME 7

DORSET

Jeffery Grayer

NOODLE BOOKS

© Kevin Robertson (Noodle Books) and Jeffery Grayer 2014

ISBN 978 1 909328 12 9

Printed in England by Berforts Information Press

First published in 2014 by Kevin Robertson under the
NOODLE BOOKS imprint

PO Box 279, Corhampton, SOUTHAMPTON. SO32 3ZX

www.noodlebooks.co.uk

The maps on pages 4 and 77 are reproduced with the kind permission of the Ordnance Survey. Unless otherwise stated, all images are by the author.

CONTENTS

Front Cover - With the background of the brooding remains of the "sleighted" Corfe Castle, the equally "sleighted" trackbed of the former Swanage branch passes under the armless gaze of a signal post. Against the odds, rails and trains returned to Corfe Castle in 1995 twenty three years after closure by BR. It is now a thriving scene with the very real prospect of a regular through service from the mainline junction at Wareham.

Frontispiece - Bucking and swaying around the curve on the approach to Maiden Newton station in the final year of the branch's existence, a single car DMU so typical of the operation of the Bridport branch in latter years, prepares to slow prior to its stop at the junction station where passengers can change for services to Dorchester, Weymouth, Yeovil and Bristol.

Opposite - Seen from under the former overall roof, adorning the Bridport bay platform at Maiden Newton, Ivatt tank No. 41284 performs a run round manoevre during the operation of the "Bridport Belle" LCGB railtour of 27th. January 1966. Classmate No. 41307 was also involved in hauling the train along the branch.

Right - 'Bubble-car' B132 passing the distant signal for Maiden Newton (Bridport branch), 19 April 1975. (Mark B Warburton)

Rear cover - BR engine - GWR Coach - Southern branch line: No 41216 coming off Cannington viaduct on the Lyme Regis branch, 3 March 1965. (Mark B Warburton)

INTRODUCTION

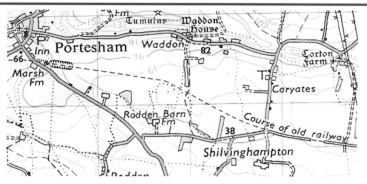

"**Course of old railway**" runs the legend on an OS map and today a dotted line on a map may be all that is left of the railway, so effectively have some lines been erased from the landscape. This, the seventh volume in the series, follows on from coverage of Hampshire, Sussex, Wiltshire, Devon, Somerset and Cornwall and features the county of Dorset. Dorset was host to perhaps one of the last true branch lines, that from Maiden Newton to Bridport which, against the odds, managed to survive until 1975. Today rails have returned to the whole length of the Swanage branch and the prospect of regular through trains from the junction at Wareham cannot, one hopes, be far from realisation with the recent announcement of a £1.47m grant leading to the prospect of through trains from Wareham in 2014. Rails have also returned to a short stretch of the S&D at Shillingstone.

For those readers wondering why, in view of the county covered by this volume, the Somerset & Dorset Joint line has only scant coverage, may I direct your attention to my previous books "**Sabotaged & Defeated**", "**Sabotaged & Defeated – Revisited**" and "**Sabotaged & Defeated – A Final Glimpse**" all of which dealt with this route in some detail. Although Volume 1 of "**Impermanent Ways**" covered a couple of lines partly in Dorset, those from Salisbury – West Moors, which also featured briefly in Volume 3, and from Brockenhurst – Wimborne and Broadstone some further images have come to light of these lines and they are included here. Whilst many of the images were taken by the author I would like to express my gratitude to those other photographers whose work appears in these pages.

Right - The rusting remains of the Weymouth Harbour tramway whose future remains in doubt following cessation of regular rail services in 1987 and occasional other uses in 1999. In January 2009 it was reported that the local Council wished to remove the tramway, and that Network Rail had confirmed it had no wish for its retention. In February 2009, the council agreed to purchase the line from Network Rail for £50,000, prior to a final decision on its future. In October 2011 it was announced that the lines were to be filled in as a safety measure. The council will use a tar and sand mix to infill the rails then cap it with a crack sealant. The treatment would stop cyclists skidding and getting their wheels stuck. The process is reversible so the rails can be brought back into use.

Jeffery Grayer   Devon 2014

HAMWORTHY GOODS

Top - The station building and platforms still remain at Hamworthy (Goods) in this view taken in the 1970s. The first standard gauge railway laid in Dorset was the Hamworthy Branch line to Poole's first station which was built in 1846 and opened to passengers in June 1847. Passenger services ceased on the 1st of July 1896 as the `New' and current Poole Station (opened in 1872) had taken over passenger services. The Hamworthy branch was singled on 25th November 1905, the remaining line serving Poole's ferry terminal and Hamworthy Quay and it was in occasional use carrying scrap metal and a small amount of freight traffic until recently. However there has been no rail traffic now for several months, the "Solent Witness" Railtour from London which also traversed lines in Southampton Docks and the Fawley branch, did visit the branch in December 2012 topped and tailed by 66201 and 66007. It was announced that this could be the last train to visit Hamworthy Goods as stone traffic had finished 3 months previously.

Bottom - A spot of bother at Hamworthy Goods where a bogie bolster wagon has been derailed on a tight curve in 1979. (Mike Couchman)

A visiting railtour disgorges its passengers at Hamworthy Goods who wander around the site. This "Dorset Venturer" railtour, run by the Poole Grammar School Railway Society, was propelled down the branch by Crompton 6528 with 4TC set 403 on 18th. September 1971. It also visited the Swanage and Wimborne lines during the tour. (Mike Couchman)

Ivatt tank No. 41275 is seen taking the Hamworthy Goods branch at Hamworthy Junction and again at Hamworthy Goods in the summer of 1965. The area of sea in the background has since been reclaimed for building the Channel Ferry Terminal. (Both Peter Russell)

Right - The old order at Wareham in 1967 with the signalbox and level crossing gates still in use and oil tankers parked in the sidings predating the installation of the oil pipeline. Two Cromptons were present in the sidings, which were the site of the original 1847 station. Of particular note is the Goods Shed set at an angle to the main running lines. (Peter Russell)

This page, left - A study in shadow as a 3H unit waits for Swanage Branch custom at Wareham, on 9th. December 1971. (John Vaughan courtesy RailPhotoprints)

Opposite top - BRC & W Type 3 6525 (33109) chatters away from Wareham with a Waterloo - Weymouth service while 3H unit 1125 waits in the bay platform with a Swanage branch service on 9th. December 1971. (John Vaughan courtesy RailPhotoprints)

Opposite bottom - The branch signal is off in this driver's eye view as a Class 3H Hampshire unit (later Class 205) approaches Worgret Junction with a Wareham - Swanage service 9th. December 1971. (John Vaughan courtesy Rail PhotoPrints)

Left - Approaching from the Swanage direction, the driver prepares to surrender the single line token. Note the 10 mph speed restriction applying at the junction. The box was closed in May 1976.

Bottom - The Worgret Junction signalman, Eddie Brown, holds up the tablet in its leather pouch and hoop ready for collection by a Wareham - Swanage service as it takes the single line to Swanage on 9th December 1971. (John Vaughan courtesy RailPhotoPrints)

Two views of the sidings at Furzebrook taken in May 1977. An exchange siding with the local china clay producer, Pike Bros., had been put in on the south side of the line. Despatch of clay continued from here until 1982. In 1978 sidings were laid on the north side to serve the Wytch Farm oilfield. (Peter Russell)

Just three weeks before the cessation of service an unidentified 3H DEMU is seen crossing over the 4-arch Portland stone viaduct to the north of Corfe Castle station which crosses the road to Studland and the Corfe river. (John Vaughan courtesy RailPhotoPrints)

The castle mound made an ideal vantage point to watch the trains go by on the branch and here a blue liveried 3-car "Thumper" unit proceeds northwards from Corfe Castle through the deep chalk cutting descending the bank at a gradient of 1 in 88.

Above - A further panoramic view taken from the castle mound with the charming village of Corfe Castle nestling in the valley bottom with the equally delightful station visible in the centre of this shot.

Right - A stark contrast with the cover picture of this book shows the line very much in operation albeit in "basic railway" format as a 3 car unit enters the station at Corfe Castle passing the up starter this time, of course, complete with signal arm.

CORFE CASTLE   p. 299, K 4
  P T EC-Thurs
Telephone   Corfe Castle 247

Ticket Office Open
          Weekdays 0715–2130
          Sundays 0950–1810

Fares to London
          1st Cl. Single 51s 9d
          2nd Cl. Single 34s 6d
          Off Peak Return 35s 6d
          Quarterly Season £55 10s 0d
Fastest journey time to London 170 mins.

Opposite top - Corfe in its neglected years shows the passage of time and the encroachment of nature onto the trackbed. The station lay dormant from closure on 3rd. January 1972 until 10th August 1991 when preserved T9 No. 120 was the first locomotive to pass over the relaid track through the station.

Opposite bottom - A work stained and grimy Standard Class 4 No. 76013 runs into Corfe as the signalman stands ready to receive the token on 27 May 1966.   (Derek Fear)

This page, top - Ivatt tank No. 41224, a regular performer on the Swanage branch, pulls away from Corfe Castle on 27 May 1966. (Derek Fear)

This page, bottom - Hampshire unit (3H) No. 1125 approaches Corfe Castle with a Wareham - Swanage service on 9th. December 1971. (John Vaughan courtesy Rail PhotoPrints)

Above - M7 tank No. 30052 propels its 2-coach load out of Corfe Castle on 29th. August 1963. M7s were superseded on the branch by more modern motive power the following year. (Alan Sainty Collection)

Left - Displaying headcode 98, an example of the staple motive power of the branch during the last few years runs into Corfe Castle where several passengers are waiting to board for Swanage. (Mike Couchman)

Right - Tablet and staff exchange at Corfe Castle as Unit 1125 calls with a Wareham - Swanage service. Just three weeks later on 3rd January 1972 services over the branch were withdrawn. (John Vaughan courtesy Rail PhotoPrints)

Bottom - Both platforms are in use at the Swanage terminus with an Ivatt tank No. 41224 at the head of the service in the bay platform and a Standard Class 4 running tender first at the main platform. Note the vintage motor coaches parked in the station yard. (Derek Fear)

Left - Unit 1128 prepares to return to the junction with an up service during the final months of operation of the branch.

Bottom - 41224 waits for departure time at Swanage in the summer of 1966 as the tail lamp is removed from the coaching stock by one of the loco crew.

Bottom - Passing the disused locomotive shed and barren turntable pit Unit 1124 runs in on the approach to Swanage station with a service from Wareham in 1971. (John Vaughan courtesy Rail PhotoPrints)

Timetable and Closure Notice posted on Corfe Castle station in December 1971. (John Vaughan courtesy RailPhotoPrints)

CHEAP DAY -2nd
Bournemouth (Central) (D.O.)
to
SWANAGE
via Poole
(S)
For condition see over
0655 0950

WITHDRAWAL OF RAILWAY PASSENGER SERVICE BETWEEN WAREHAM AND SWANAGE

The Southern Region of British Railways hereby give notice that on and from Monday 3 January 1972 the railway passenger service between Wareham and Swanage will be withdrawn and Corfe Castle and Swanage stations closed.

Details of the alternative bus services are available at local railway stations and bus offices.

≠ British Rail | Southern

Memories of steam days on the branch are evoked by these two views, the top picture showing M7 30107 shunting its maroon coaching stock at the terminus in September 1957. The lower view shows more modern motive power in the form of 76010 waiting to leave the terminus. (Both Alan Sainty Collection)

Top - The run round loop had been removed by the time of this shot, December 1971, as only a "basic railway" was now needed to cater for 3H Unit 1110 waiting to depart from Swanage. (John Vaughan courtesy RailPhotoPrints)

Right - Buffer stop view of Unit 1110 at Swanage. (Mike Couchman)

Waiting its time in Woodhams yard at Barry, Bulleid West Country Pacific 34105 "*Swanage*" would be the 90th. locomotive to escape the scrapyard after 13 years of exposure to the salt air. It would make a triumphant return to its namesake location in 1993 where it is seen in resplendent restored condition sporting an "Atlantic Coast Express" headboard alongside classmate 34072 "*257 Squadron*".

Right - No 37191 runs along the tramway on 4th. August 1993 with a train which was booked to run each Wednesday, utilising the locomotive and stock from the morning 09.00 Bristol Temple Meads - Weymouth Town before it returned at 16.30, between 14th July and 1st September 1993. The train was advertised by Regional Railways as a joint venture with Cherry Tree Catering under the banner "Special train through the streets of Weymouth".

Bottom - Sealink ferries, believed to be the SS Sarnia in the background and Earl Godwin in the foreground, lie tied up at Weymouth Quay on Sunday 25th. June 1978 adjacent to the platform used by boat trains. These trains operated formerly from Paddington but in later years from Waterloo via the Weymouth tramway. Sealink was a ferry company based in the UK from 1970 to 1984 when it was sold to Sea Containers Ltd. for £66m. Two boys fish from the rocks by the breakwater.

Top - Crompton 33008 "Eastleigh" is seen wending its tortuous way along the Quay tramway on 29th. June 1985 with the Hertfordshire Railtours "Pines Pullman" the stock for which, as its name suggests, consisted of a number of Pullman cars.

Left - Proceeded by flag carrying BR staff, 4TC set No. 415 displaying headcode 90 and forming an up boat train with Crompton 33115 at the rear traverses the tramway on 18th. August 1985. Cromptons began to be used regularly on the tramway from May 1973, the last summer service to Waterloo finishing in September 1987.

GWR 1366 1F class 0-6-0PT No. 1370 shunts wagons around at Weymouth Quay, alongside the ferry berths for the Channel Islands ships on Saturday 27th April 1957. (D.E White from the Geoff Plumb Collection)

GWR 1366 class 0-6-0PT No. 1367 works a passenger train, of "blood and custard" stock, along the Weymouth Quay Tramway from the harbour to the town station, having met a cross channel ferry sailing on Tuesday 30th April 1957. Notice the delightful period advertisements on the left for Chivers jellies and Woodbine cigarettes. (D.E White from the Geoff Plumb Collection)

Left - A busy scene at Weymouth Quay. 33112 waits with the up Weymouth Quay - Waterloo Boat Train while Bristol based Class 117 B429 (51367, 59519, 51409) waits with a service for Bristol in June 1984. These Bristol services ran for two summer seasons in 1983 and 1984. (John Vaughan courtesy RailPhotoPrints)

Bottom - Pannier 1370 is seen again on the tramway this time in August 1959. Notice that goods are being loaded/unloaded from the lorry on the right directly to the platform. (Alan Sainty Collection)

No 6520 threads its way to Weymouth Quay with a boat train from Waterloo on 6th. October 1973. (Mark B Warburton)

Opposite top - Traffic warranted the use of two locomotives in this view taken on 29th. July 1961. 9626 is on the right whilst another pannier can be seen in the left background. An Austin A35 and wharf cranes complete the period scene. (Alan Sainty Collection)

Opposite bottom - 1369 is seen in this undated view shunting coaching stock at the Quayside terminus. Three of the panniers based here would depart for pastures new at Wadebridge in 1962 to assume control of the Wenfordbridge mineral line from the ageing Beattie well tanks.

This page - On 29 December 1979 Crompton 33102 eases its way along the quayside with the "Sulzer Surveyor 2" railtour, the Class 33 being used solely for this street running section of the tour. (Rail Photoprints)

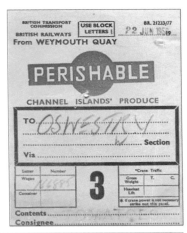

Left - Crompton 33116 is seen at the Quay station with the 15:50 service to Waterloo on 21st April 1975. (Derek Fear)

Bottom - Weymouth Quay on 8th July 1979 plays host to 33104 and the Great Western Society 'Vintage Train' in appropriate brown and cream livery. (Derek Fear)

Pages 225-227—WEYMOUTH TO WEYMOUTH QUAY—continued

Additional Instructions for the Working of Passenger Trains on the Tramway.

Passenger trains must be drawn in both directions, and the Shunter-in-Charge must walk in front of each train throughout the Tramway.

The load of each train must not exceed the equivalent of 12 coaches (viz. 96 wheels).

Buffers of coaching stock must not be less than 1 foot 6 inches in width.

Coaching stock, except auto-coupled stock for which see below, exceeding the following dimensions is prohibited:—

63 feet 6 inches in length over buffers by 9 feet 3 inches in width over body.

64 feet 6 inches in length over buffers by 9 feet 0 inches in width over body.

W.R. stock 66 feet 8 inches in length over buffers by 8 feet 11 inches in width over body.

Non-corridor sets permanently close coupled together by special type buffing and drawgear are prohibited.

Automatic coupled corridor stock not exceeding 67 feet 1 inch in length over extended buffers and 9 feet 3 inches extreme width may work to Weymouth Quay provided gangway curtains are fitted on all occasions.

When a down passenger train is required to run between Weymouth Station and the Quay it must be brought to a stand at Nicholas Street by day, or opposite Webb-Major's timber yard by night, if it cannot be confirmed before the train leaves Weymouth Station that the Tramway line is clear to the Quay.

When there are engines or trains on the Quay side of Nicholas Street, such engines or trains must be placed clear of the Tramway and must remain in that position until after the passenger train has passed the point concerned. The Shunter in charge of such engines or trains must, after the engines or trains have been placed clear of the Tramway instruct the Drivers not to move their engines. Whenever a train or engine has been placed into a Siding the Shunter-in-Charge must then personally pilot the passenger train past the siding concerned. The engines or trains must not be allowed to proceed on to the Tramway again until it is safe to do so. A down passenger train must not proceed beyond Nicholas Street until the Shunter in charge of any other engines or trains, which have been placed clear of the Tramway, has joined it except as shown in the following paragraph.

A second or subsequent passenger trains may follow a passenger train from Weymouth Station to the Quay at an interval of not less than 10 minutes by day or 15 minutes by night. In such circumstances the second or subsequent trains must stop at Nicholas Street by day or opposite Webb-Major's timber yard by night and await the arrival of the Shunter-in-Charge of the preceding passenger train before proceeding to the Quay. When the Shunter-in-Charge is required to return to Nicholas Street or opposite Webb-Major's timber yard, as the case may be, to accompany a following passenger train, he must instruct the Driver of his train that he must not move his engine on to the Tramway until permission is given, also come to a clear understanding with the Shunters in charge of any other engines or trains in sidings that they must not obstruct the Tramway, and then return as quickly as possible to Nicholas Street or opposite Webb-Major's timber yard, as the case may be, and pilot the next passenger train to the Quay.

An up passenger train from the Quay to Weymouth Station must not be allowed to leave the Quay until the Shunter-in-Charge has satisfied himself that no conflicting movement is being or about to be made and that the Tramway line is clear of engines and railway vehicles. A second or subsequent passenger trains may follow a passenger train at an interval of 10 minutes by day or 15 minutes by night.

The Shunter in charge of the working of a passenger train, and the Guard, must prevent passengers from alighting whenever a passenger train is brought to a stand on the Tramway.

When it is necessary to work a passenger train to, from or through the cargo stage loop, the points leading into the loop must be securely wedged and the lever working the points must be firmly held by the man appointed by the person in charge of the cargo stage, while the whole of the train passes into, from or through the loop.

The front van should be used, when necessary, for passengers' luggage, etc.

The above instructions supersede the temporary instructions issued by the District Traffic Superintendent (Southampton) on Special Circulars Nos. 4203 (13/5/1961) and 4213 (24/7/1961) and by the District Traffic Manager (Southampton) on Special Circular No. 4239 (20/3/1962).

(LM—SW/R/SA/82)

WEYMOUTH OLD STATION *Rebuilt 1986*

Left - A 1979 view of the, by this time increasingly decrepit, old station at Weymouth with Crompton 33111 on push pull duties to Bournemouth and a DMU on a Bristol service. The final remains of the former station were demolished in 1986

Bottom - 34004 formerly named "Yeovil" double heading with a Crompton awaits departure time from the old station at Weymouth on 6th. July 1967. (George Woods)

RADIPOLE HALT

Closed 6-2-1984

Above - Radipole station looking north in March 1983. The station lighting and signs have now been upgraded, and since 1978 the old GWR pagoda shelters have been replaced with modern bus shelters. Trains stopped calling at Radipole nine months after this picture was taken - because of the poor condition of the platforms - and the station was officially closed on 6 February 1984, the last train calling on 31st. December 1963. (Nick Catford)

Right - A southbound train from London to Weymouth headed by 75079 steams through Radipole Halt in April 1966. This Standard was withdrawn in November the same year and passed into preservation being currently housed on the Mid Hants Railway. (Brian Robbins courtesy RailPhotoPrints)

UPWEY WISHING WELL HALT *Closed 7-1-1957*

34019 "Bideford" storms through Upwey Wishing Well halt with a Waterloo train on 26 May 1966. (Derek Fear)

Crompton 33113 propelling a London service north through the increasingly grass grown platforms of the former Upwey Wishing Well Halt in 1981. Such scenes would continue until electrification of the route in May 1988.

35008 "Orient Line" climbs the bank through the former Upwey Wishing Well halt before entering the most southerly of the two Bincombe Tunnels, this being 48 yards long whilst its northerly neighbour is 819 yards in length. Although undated this was right towards the very end of steam, the engine having been lovingly polished ready for the one of the official 'end of steam' runs but minus nameplates. (George Woods)

Opposite top - A mixed motive power scene captured on 8 August 1965 with a Crompton, parked adjacent to a couple of oil tankers, sharing the shed with steam in the shape of a brace of Bulleid Pacifics in the foreground and by the coaling stage to the right. The 'Bulleid' nearest the camera, possibly No 34082, is temporarily out of service under repair having had the rear set of driving wheels removed.(Derek Fear)

Opposite bottom - 34095 "Brentor" runs off shed on 8 August 1965 towards the station. (Derek Fear)

This page top - 35022 "Holland-America" line is parked adjacent to the Weymouth Breakdown train at the rear of the shed on 26 May 1966. (Derek Fear)

This page bottom - A Crompton seen in company with Standards 73016 and 76006 together with original and rebuilt Bulleid Pacifics at Weymouth shed on 26 May 1966. (Derek Fear)

Left - Merchant Navy 35014 "Nederland Line" is seen on shed alongside another Bulleid carrying a red "Not to be Moved" board on its tender in the dying days of steam.

Bottom - The rusty wheels of 73016 belies the reasonable condition of the cabside and tender and indicates that this locomotive has not been moved for some time having been parked at the rear of the shed since withdrawal in December 1966. The locomotive had been delivered new in 1951 to Sheffield Grimesthorpe and after spells at Sheffield Millhouses, Derby and Canklow moved to the SR at the end of 1964.

Right - A brace of Ivatt tanks 41230 and 41295 form part of the melancholy lines of withdrawn locomotives at Weymouth dump following the end of SR steam in July 1967.

Bottom - Rebuilt Bulleid Pacifics, "West Country" class No. 34009 "Lyme Regis" on the left and "Battle of Britain" class No. 34077 "603 Squadron" are being serviced at Weymouth MPD in between duties on Sunday 6th February 1966. Both locos are absolutely filthy but at least still carry their nameplates. (From the Geoff Plumb Collection of original slides. Photo by Mike Burnett.)

Above - Filthy dirty BR Standard 5MT 4-6-0 No. 73002 stands in the yard at Weymouth shed between duties, on Sunday 6th February 1966. (From the Geoff Plumb Collection of original slides. Photo by Mike Burnett.)

Left - A deserted shed seen in 1969. Weymouth remained a signing on point until October 1970 with all sidings being taken out of use in November of that year.

ABBOTSBURY BRANCH

Closed 1-12-1952

Right - Seen through the glassless windows of the closed Upwey & Broadwey Signal Box, this was the former junction for the branchline to Abbotsbury. The box closed in March 1970. The station, originally called Upwey, was resited and renamed Upwey Junction shortly after the opening of the Abbotsbury branch in 1885 and was then renamed Upwey & Broadwey upon closure of the branch and became plain Upwey again in May 1980.

Bottom - The box is still open for business in this view of 73019 with a 3 coach local taken on 26 May 1966. (Derek Fear)

Above - Green liveried King Arthur Class 30806 "Sir Galleron " rolls into Upwey in the summer of 1959. Thomas Hardy wrote a short poem based here entitled "At the railway station, Upway" (sic) in which a convict and accompanying policeman are waiting for a train whilst a boy lightens the felon's mood by playing his violin. (Alan Sainty Collection)

Left - Upwey, the first station on the Abbotsbury branch, remained open for freight until 1st. January 1962, the rest of the branch having been lifted by 1955. Track to Upwey was removed about 1965. The view was taken in the late 1960s and shows the growth of vegetation both on the platforms and former permanent way.

Above - Looking west at Upwey in March 1984. The site was occupied by the firm of "I J House – Roofing" between 1977 – 1994. The station site is currently occupied by 'Buildrite' a trade builders and roofing merchant and DIY and hire shop and is still run by the House family. The former Goods Shed here is now used as a cash and carry collection point. (Nick Catford)

Right - Much remains at Portesham station in this view taken in December 2012. The Goods Shed is on the left and the platform and station building, sadly devoid of its canopy, is on the right and has been refurbished as "Sleepers" a holiday let. (Nick Catford)

Above - Looking in the opposite direction the new bungalow built on the trackbed in the distance belongs to the landowner. (Nick Catford)

Opposite top - A closer look at Portesham Goods Shed reveals that the loading gauge is still in situ and can be seen beyond the greenhouse. (Nick Catford)

Opposite bottom - Abbotsbury goods shed looking east in December 2011. The line passed to the left of the goods shed and the photographer is standing on the site of the former cattle dock siding. (Nick Catford)

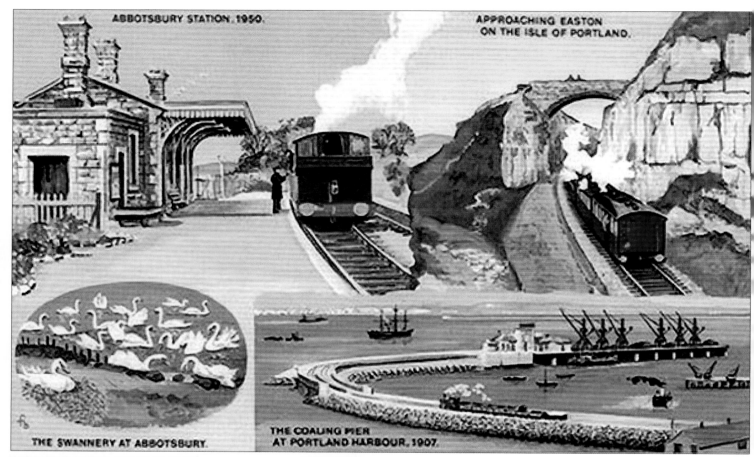

ABBOTSBURY STATION. 1950.

APPROACHING EASTON ON THE ISLE OF PORTLAND.

THE SWANNERY AT ABBOTSBURY.

THE COALING PIER AT PORTLAND HARBOUR, 1907.

Dereliction at Abbotsbury with the base of the former water tower on the left and the engine shed, now sporting a corrugated iron sheet roof, in the centre of this view. The base of the water tower used to house a small steam pump to raise water from a nearby well. Steam for this was provided by the branch locomotive by means of a flexible pipe coupled in place of one of the whistles. Water from here was also used to flush the station lavatories. The shed was closed soon after the line was absorbed by the GWR in 1896 however, it is not recorded as being out of use until 1906.

The remains of Melcombe Regis platform seen in March 1983. Although the station officially closed on 3rd. March 1952 it was retained as a summer Saturdays overflow for the main Weymouth station until 12th. May 1959. (Nick Catford)

Happier times at Melcombe Regis as pannier tank 3737 calls with the RCTS "Greyhound" tour on 14th. August 1960. The pannier operated the leg from here to Easton and return, passengers having to make their way to and from the main Weymouth station where Drummond Greyhound No. 30718 was the motive power. (Alan Sainty Collection)

Westham crossing box and platform seen in June 1968 with track still in place albeit very grass grown. (Peter Russell)

Top - The platform at the former Wyke Regis halt which formerly housed a typical GWR pagoda tin shelter is still visible. Opened in 1909 the platform was lengthened in 1913. It was situated near the Whitehead Torpedo Works which had a pier with its own tramway for carrying torpedoes to waiting ships. Whitehead's expertise led to the Royal Naval establishment at Portland becoming a major anti-submarine and torpedo warfare centre in both the First and Second World Wars. The Whitehead site is now a housing estate.

Right - The platforms of Rodwell Halt can be seen when walking or cycling the 2 ¼ mile Rodwell Trail. Replica totem signs have now been erected on the platform.

Two views taken in the late 1960s of Rodwell Halt with the very overgrown track still in situ . Goods services to Portland finished in April 1965 but the track remained until recovery a few years later.

BRITISH RAILWAYS (S)
RODWELL
PLATFORM TICKET 1d.
Available ONE HOUR on Day of Issue only
NOT VALID IN TRAINS NOT TRANSFERABLE
To be given up when leaving Platform
FOR CONDITIONS SEE BACK

3233

S.2 G.W. & SOUTHERN Ry⁵
The holder is Prohibited from
entering the Company's Trains
Not Transferable
Admit ONE to PLATFORM 1ᴰ
Available ONE HOUR on DAY of
ISSUE ONLY
This Ticket must be given up on
leaving Platform

FOR CONDITIONS SEE BACK

PORTLAND

0800

Easton station, terminus of passenger services from Weymouth. Easton was closed from 1941 to 1944, except during the summer months, due to wartime restrictions. Regular freight continued after passenger closure in 1952 until the mid 1960s. The former station survived for a number of years devoid of its canopy but is now the site of Ladymead Hall a residential home for the elderly.

0024

S. & G.W.Rlys.(E.& C.H.)
PRIVILEGE TICKET.
Available for One Month
including Day of issue and return
Issued subject to the conditions
(a) on the Privilege Ticket Order
and (b) on the back hereof

Easton to
PORTLAND
Third Class

S. & G.W.Rlys.(E.& C.H.)
PRIVILEGE TICKET.
Available for One Week
including Day of issue

Portland
Easton

Portland to
EASTON
Third Class

0024

Pannier tank 7782 runs round at Easton whilst working the SCTS "Southern Counties Enterprise" railtour in conjunction with 4689 on 25th August 1963. The tanks operated the leg from Weymouth Junction to Easton and return continuing on to Maiden Newton for a trip over the Bridport branch. Most unusually A3 Pacific 60112 "St. Simon" then took the tour to Waterloo.

2nd SPECIAL EXCURSION

SOUTHERN COUNTIES TOURING
SOCIETY
SOUTHERN COUNTIES ENTERPRISE
(C.M.168) SUNDAY 25th. AUG. 1963

Waterloo to WATERLOO
Via Hamworthy Goods, Easton, West Bay, Westbury, Wylye & East Putney
(S)   (S)
FOR CONDITIONS SEE OVER

0266   0266

DORCHESTER

Right - Dorchester Junction signalbox lay in the convergence of the lines from Bournemouth in the foreground and from Yeovil behind the box. It is seen here on 2nd. September 1976 and was to close in June 1985. The nameboard from the box was sold at auction in 2010 for £350.

Bottom - The green enamel running in board, a remnant of SR responsibility for the station which dates from 1950, still survives in this view of the station at Dorchester West. It became unstaffed in January 1972 and remains open today for services from Weymouth to Yeovil and Bristol.

Top - The necessity for up trains to reverse at Dorchester was a legacy of the original intention to continue west from the station towards Exeter. This convoluted arrangement persisted for over a century, as witness a rather grimy 34012 'Launceston' slowing on the approach after which it will pull forward and reverse into the platform. 26 March 1966.
(Mark B Warburton)

Bottom - The former up platform at Dorchester South seen on a wintry day in 1986. Following the provision of a second platform sited on the curve to Weymouth the operational nightmare of backing eastbound trains into the old platform ceased in 1970. The buildings on the trackless original platform remained in use until 1989 and as part of the modernisation work preparatory to electrification a new booking hall was built on the curved platform, replacing the building on the original platform which was then demolished. A wooden walkway can be seen crossing the trackbed giving access to the new platform.

MAIDEN NEWTON - BRIDPORT Closed 5-5-1975
BRIDPORT - WEST BAY Closed 22-9-1930

Maiden Newton was all about passenger interchange and this can be seen being amply demonstrated in this view of a Cardiff bound DMU connecting with the single unit railcar forming a departure to Bridport in 1974. Sadly the overall roof originally provided for the bay had gone by this time as had the original lattice style footbridge to be replaced by a SR style concrete version.

The Bridport train gingerly makes its way out of the station to round the curve under the bridge. Note the 10 mph speed restriction applying. Note also the singling of the mainline northwards which had been accomplished in 1968. The GWR built house for the station master in on the left.

Left - A busy scene at Maiden Newton as northbound loco hauled stock and a southbound DMU cross each other on the single line section from Yeovil to Dorchester in the early 1970s. The 57 lever signalbox dating from 1921 was still operating at this time, not closing until 1988. It was subsequently used as a pw depot.

Bottom - Long evening shadows creep across this delightful Dorset pastoral scene in the mid 1980s, the sun still illuminating the signalbox and the refuge siding maintained for the use of engineers. The heaps of coal were not alas delivered by rail by this time but arrived by road for the local coal merchant. The view is looking north towards Yeovil and Castle Cary.

Unusual motive power in the shape of Black 5 45493 coupled ahead of Bulleid Pacific 34100 "Appledore" pause at the station for a photographic stop whilst heading the LCGB "Green Arrow" railtour of 3rd July 1966. Unfortunately "Green Arrow" brought down especially from Dundee failed. This pair of locomotives handled the leg from Salisbury – Yeovil Junction – Yeovil Pen Mill – Weymouth. The knapped flint Goods Shed, which formerly housed a 30cwt crane, can be seen on the left.

Top - Pannier tank 4689 shunts a solitary coach at Maiden Newton on 26th. September 1960 whilst two railwaymen take an interest in the photographer. The Goods Shed complete with a couple of trucks is seen to advantage in this view. (Alan Sainty Collection)

Middle - Seen from the hill overlooking the railway on the east side of the line the railway blends perfectly into the landscape. The Bridport line would head off west on the right hand side of the station.

Bottom - A Swindon built Class 120 DMU leads another 3 car set into Maiden Newton in September 1971 sporting the destination blind "Weymouth Town". (John A. M. Vaughan courtesy RailPhotoPrints)

Top - Looking south from the down platform with the main station building constructed from the same knapped flint. The station featured in an episode of the TV series 'To the Manor Born'.(Sean Bolan)

Middle - A midwinter scene at a deserted Maiden Newton station as W55032 sits in the Bridport Bay platform awaiting custom in December 1972. (John A. M. Vaughan courtesy RailPhotoPrints)

Bottom - W55032 makes a smoky exit from Maiden Newton as it leaves for Bridport on a frosty December morning in 1972. It will be apparent that access to the branch prevented through running following junction alterations carried out in April 1968. (John A. M. Vaughan courtesy RailPhotoPrints)

Top - An earlier view of the fully signalled layout at Maiden Newton showing that Bridport trains could run through to the main line without the need for reversal. The site of the former gravity siding, for shunting coaches clear of the bay platform to allow the locomotive to run round, can be seen on the right adjacent to the wartime concrete tank traps. The Southern influence, in the form of the upper quadrant signals, on what had until 1950 been a (G)WR route, will be noted. (M Boddy)

Left - Following the arrival of the Weymouth service, the Bridport unit will shortly leave on its 9¼ mile journey taking some 18 minutes. (Derek Fear)

Right - On the last day of service on the Bridport branch, 5th. May 1975, a strengthened train consisting of single unit W55033 leading a 3 coach DMU rounds the curve on the approach to Maiden Newton. (John A. M. Vaughan courtesy RailPhotoPrints)

Bottom - Running into the bay platform at Maiden Newton a single car on 2nd May 1975 a few days before the end. (Derek Fear)

PASSENGERS ARE REQUESTED TO CROSS THE LINE BY THE BRIDGE

A LONG TIME A–DYING

The Bridport Line proved to be Dorset's last operational branch and remarkably survived closure attempts for more than 15 years before finally succumbing to the inevitable in 1975.

As an elderly Bedford OB coach, registration HOD 76, of 1949 vintage resplendent in the colours of local operator Pearce & Co. of Cattistock, ground its way out of the station approach at Maiden Newton on the morning of Monday 5 May 1975 a new era in public transport in this area of West Dorset had begun. This was the first day of a rail replacement bus service covering the route of Dorset's last passenger branch line which had closed down after nearly 118 years of

operation the previous Saturday night. The twenty nine seats of the Bedford were soon to be replaced by 17/20 seat minibuses which were more suited to the winding country lanes of the district and the dwindling number of former rail passengers willing to make the trek by road. These same lanes had been instrumental in prolonging the life of the branch which had resisted all closure attempts since the early 1960s.

This was a far cry from the halcyon days of 1959 when the introduction of diesel multiple units was hailed as the saviour of ailing branch lines and this was very much the hope in rural Dorset when on 6 April regular diesel services started on the branch, initially with 3 trains daily, as part of the Bristol Area Diesel Scheme. Complete dieselisation of the branch, with the exception of two trips daily worked by the branch goods engine, followed on 15 June although the 3 car sets used initially were subsequently replaced by 2 car sets and ultimately by single units indicating graphically the declining usage of the line over the years. Nonetheless back in the 1950's it looked as if the branch had a secure future. This was borne out by a Southern Region Branch Lines Committee Report of 1954 (page 68/69) which concluded that based on figures for 1950 the line was "**economically sound and it is therefore recommended that it be retained.**" Annual income from passenger and freight business was reckoned at £195,289 with annual savings from closure yielding only £60,544 although a liability of £2,275 p.a. for fencing and "disinfestations" until the land could be sold and £35,255 for heavy items of repairs and renewals in the next 10 years if the line were to be kept open, needed to be taken into account. Notwithstanding these, the branch appeared to be turning in a healthy profit, the only action being deemed necessary at the time was the removal of redundant sidings at Powerstock !

After arrival of the diesel sets, steam continued for a while with goods trains and with one remaining steam hauled passenger turn. Until the introduction of Ivatt tanks to Weymouth at the end of 1963, ex GWR 57XX pannier tanks and 45XX tanks monopolised these services. These had held sway since the end of World War II with the occasional appearance of a 74XX tank to add variety to the motive power scene. The sub shed at Bridport closed with the introduction of diesels, the last locomotives leaving on the morning of 15th. June 1959 being 4507 and 4562. Since the introduction of diesels steam had occasionally made forays down the branch with a number of special workings and a pair of Ivatts, 41295 and 41320, were in fact to haul the last steam train on the branch when, with the ill fated LCGB special "The Bridport Belle" on January 22nd.1967, they famously stalled in heavy rain in the notorious Witherstone cutting and had to be rescued by Crompton diesel D6541. Having been controlled by the GWR since 1901, the branch naturally fell within the Western Region orbit following nationalisation. However, in April 1950 the Bridport branch and the mainline between Sparkford and Weymouth transferred from WR to SR control although the shed at Weymouth (82F) remained under the control of the WR until 1959 when it was transferred to the SR and coded 71G. In January 1963 the Bridport branch and the mainline between the north end of Poundbury tunnel, Dorchester and Sparkford were transferred back to the WR. This was part of the scheme which handed all SR controlled lines west of Salisbury to the WR. However, in the case of the Bridport branch the locomotives, diesel units, drivers and guards were still supplied by the SR from Weymouth depot

Although 13 trains a day each way and 8 on Sundays were provided on the 9¼ mile branch in 1960 and the level of freight was reasonably healthy, all was not as well as it might be at the start of the new decade. In November 1961 the Committee for the Review of Uneconomic Branch Lines and Stations, to give it its full title, met in London to discuss amongst other lines

Opposite - End of an era, the Closure Notice for the branch. (Derek Fear)

Above - The idyll that was Toller station photographed from the lane serving the chocolate box cottage and garden to match on the right and formerly the Goods Depot, a reminder of which is provided by the moribund sign on the left. The road also crossed the line on the level before the provision of the adjacent bridge.

the Bridport branch. It was stated at this meeting that the " **introduction of a diesel service has had no measurable effect on passenger travel on this line**", as had been the case elsewhere on many lines where increases of several hundred percent had been registered. It was mentioned that an enquiry envisaging withdrawal of the passenger train service had been convened the previous year on 6 October 1960. The Committee heard the ominous news that the Chief Accountant was preparing revenue figures up to the end of September 1961 and that details of the Chief Civil Engineer's savings were awaited. In the summer of 1962 the Sunday service was reduced to 7 trains each way but the introduction of the winter service saw Sunday services withdrawn altogether and the daily service reduced to 11. The Loders branch of the local W.I. had got wind of the uncertainty hanging over the branch's future and had written to the local MP, the gloriously named Simon Wingfield Digby, in October asking for his help in ensuring the branch remained open. The MP duly wrote to Dr Beeching but received only the blandest of non committal replies. On the 3rd December the line from Bridport to West Bay closed to goods, having closed to passengers as far back as 1930, the extension never having fulfilled the hopes of its promoters. During the severe winter of 1962/63 the branch was hailed as a lifeline for passengers and goods alike with many roads being blocked for considerable periods. The start of the New Year saw the branch transferred from SR to WR responsibility – always a bad sign for the future of a line !

Not surprisingly the publication of the Beeching Report on 27 March 1963 proposed the Bridport branch for complete closure with all stations between Yeovil Pen Mill and Dorchester West, amazingly including the latter, on the main line listed for closure to passengers. There followed a dramatic reduction to 8 trains per day on the branch from 6 April 1964, BR claiming that the less well patronised services had been "weeded out" - often a euphemism for making a line as unattractive as possible to passengers. This was followed on 1st September by the posting of proposals for closure of all intermediate stations on the main line between Yeovil and Dorchester including Maiden Newton which of course still served the Bridport branch but for which incongruously no separate closure procedure had been initiated. A Public Enquiry was held at Yetminster on 25th November 1964 resulting in the Minister's decision given on 22nd April 1965 announcing that Maiden Newton and Dorchester would remain open as would Yetminster, Thornford and Chetnole, but that all other remaining stations on the main line would close on 3rd October 1966.

Further retrenchment took place on 8 June 1965 when all surplus trackwork and sidings on the branch together with Bridport signal box were taken out of use. The staff at Bridport was reduced to just 3 where it had been 25 only a year previously. The line was becoming very much a "basic railway" with train guards having to open and close the only set of level crossing gates on the line at Bradpole, but this was the price to pay if economies were to be achieved and the line stay in business. As a consequence of this crossing gate manoeuvre and the introduction of single car units the previous journey time of 18 minutes achieved when diesel multiple units were first introduced was increased to 22 minutes. On 3 October 1965 BR (WR) announced a proposed closure date of one year hence claiming an operating loss of £9,314 p.a. on the line. A public enquiry into the closure was held in West Bay convened by the Transport Users Consultative Committee (TUCC) for the South East on 5 April 1966. The scope of the many objections covered the usefulness of the line during the "Great Freeze" of 1962/63; the considerable number of students using the line daily; the unsuitability of the local country roads to carry any replacement bus services and the considerable cost involved in upgrading them. There was also of course the general caveat regarding the adverse effect on the tourist and holiday trade of the area not to mention the detrimental effect on any future expansion of Bridport as a thriving market town.

Rather late in the day, 11 April 1966 in fact, the intermediate stations of Toller and Powerstock were reduced to unstaffed halts. It is rather surprising that this obvious economy was not introduced earlier in view of the ability of conductor guards carried by the single diesel units to issue tickets. This action saved the princely sum of £900 p.a. in terminal expenses ! On 4 July 1966 the Minister of Transport said the branch must stay open, Barbara Castle stressing that the 100 people who used the line every day would have to use buses as an alternative and that bus journeys over winding roads would take 50 as against 22 minutes by rail. She also said that delays and hardship would result and that the considerable expenditure on local roads required to bring them up to the standard for replacement buses would outweigh the small financial benefit of closure. It was felt unlikely that Dorset County Council would pay the £53,000 required for the necessary road improvements, In 1968 the main line was reduced to single track between Castle Cary and Dorchester with passing loops retained at Yeovil Pen Mill and at Maiden Newton. The junction of the Bridport branch with the mainline was also simplified thereby preventing through running to Dorchester, all trains having to reverse in the bay platform to gain the up mainline. By the end of 1969 the last member of BR staff left Bridport, the canopy over the branch bay was removed at Maiden Newton, the steel footbridge replaced here by a second-hand concrete one, the junction station also becoming unstaffed with only a signalman in attendance.

On 11 June 1971 BR tried again and gave notice of closure claiming a loss which by now had reached £12,000 p.a. A traffic census was undertaken on 19/20 October and reflected the traffic levels noted by a correspondent to the Railway Observer on 16 September when the 1249 service from Maiden Newton carried only 6 passengers and the 1355 return only 5 with a negligible level of intervening traffic. On 22 March 1972 a public enquiry was held at Bridport, the 19 strong panel reviewed the 97 written objections, considered a petition of 72 signatures, listened to objections from 15 interested parties delivered in person during a meeting, attended by 80 people, which lasted 1.5 hours. Naturally the County Council was firmly opposed to the closure with the same arguments being advanced that had been used previously concerning the inadequate state of the country roads to take replacement bus services. BR said that the average number of passengers per day had plummeted by nearly 50% between 1965 and 1971 and that the loss had now escalated to £36,000 pa (Passenger figures for 1965/1970/1971 for winter and summer periods are shown on page 68). By closing the branch the wages of 3 drivers, 1 secondman, 3 guards and 3 trackmen could be saved together with the costs associated with a single power unit and upkeep of the 9.3 miles of track. Of course BR said that they did not want to close the line but the problem was that grant aid was being withdrawn. The Bridport branch was one of 222 unremunerative services for which grants were payable under the terms of the 1968 Transport Act. A two year grant was made covering 1969 and 1970 in the sum of £33,000 p.a. which compared to the Plymouth – Gunnislake grant of £103,000 for example for the same period, the latter line of course being still with us. The Minister wanted to know the result of the enquiry before considering whether the grant should be continued. In April 1972 the TUCC Interim Report said that their was no material change in the level of hardship that would be caused by closure since the earlier closure refusal and in December any decision as to the line's future was deferred. Even though closure had tentatively been set for 1 January 1973, the Minister was apparently still considering the matter. The only bus directly serving the route of the line was the Western National Route 403 from Powerstock to Bridport and back on a Friday morning.

All then went quiet until the Dorset Evening Echo announced on 3 January 1975 that "The Axe Falls on Bridport's Line". It was to close from 5 May that year the deficit now having risen to a very substantial £54,000 pa. The DoE statutory notice of closure admitted that there would be hardship if the service was withdrawn and openly stated that *"there is not and will not be a parallel bus service from Maiden Newton to Bridport and on some roads it will be virtually impossible for a minibus to pass other traffic and the routes may become impassable or dangerous in the winter"*. No additional bus services had yet been stipulated. The notice calmly stated that the train service should not be withdrawn before "*local councils and other interested bodies*" had time to consider organising additional buses. A Bridport Line Action group sprang into being to try and save the line but at this late stage nothing could be done to stave off the inevitable. According to another Railway Observer correspondent the single unit operating the service on 22 April 1975 left at 12:27 from Maiden Newton with 20 on board carrying 3 to Toller and the remaining 17 to Bridport. The return trip was no better with 15 on board the 13:55 from Bridport picking up another 3 at Powerstock. A replacement bus service of sorts was organised and, as was the case with most similar ventures, a considerable subsidy was needed to keep it going, the route passing through a number of operators' hands and seeing a progressive reduction in the number of services provided in the ensuing years.

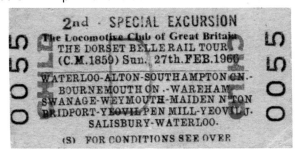

Top - The strengthened set on the final day enters Toller where more than the usual solitary passenger awaits. (John A M Vaughan courtesy RailPhotoPrints)

Bottom left - Taken from the train window as the unit halts for custom which seldom came, this is the sad sight of Toller seen in its twilight days. The station building here was rescued and re-erected at Totnes Littlehempston on the Dart Valley line.

This page - Close up of the wooden station building at Toller, boarded up since withdrawal of staff who incredibly lingered on at this remote spot until 11th. April 1966.

Opposite, bottom right - A tattered poster advertising closure of the line adorns the walls of Toller station long after the last train had gone.

Rather than face the last day crowds, I made my own final pilgrimage to the line on the penultimate Saturday, April 26 1975, when I travelled by rail from Bristol down to Maiden Newton. Here the usual single diesel unit, B132 on this occasion, was in the bay platform awaiting departure time. Even with a week to go seats were at a premium for most of the services on that Saturday. Setting off from the bay platform at the junction observing the severe 10 mph speed restriction, the unit rattled its way around the curves to reach Toller conveniently situated in the heart of the small village. The couple of passengers who got on here were outnumbered by the photographers and we were away again to Powerstock whose station was privately purchased in 1968 and subsequently converted into a B & B establishment. We halted for a third time at Bradpole level crossing where the guard opened and then closed the gates behind us after our passage across the road. Trundling into Bridport station, which by that time been unstaffed for 6 years and was showing signs of serious neglect, we shuddered to a halt. Peeling paint, the building had not been repainted for years, and boarded up windows were not an inviting prospect for the enthusiast let alone any would-be rail passengers. On the day before closure the single unit W55032 failed after which a 3-car unit took over for remainder of day. A single car unit in tandem with a 3-car unit operated the following day W55033/W51387-W59497-W51345, the 9 train service, which had been the norm for a number of years, being augmented with 2 additional departures. The final train rolled into the bay platform at Maiden Newton, where one of the station signs was decorated with the traditional wreath, just after 21:00. Shortly after, it departed, with passengers still aboard, for stations in the direction of Westbury. Thus ended rail services over Dorset's last branch after a very protracted

MAIDEN NEWTON/BRIDPORT BRANCH LINE
USE MADE OF TRAINS BY STATIONS - SUMMARY

STATIONS	Number of passengers WINTER												Number of passengers SUMMER											
	w.e. 20.1.1965				w.e. 24.10.1970				w.e. 6.11.1971				w.e. 10.7.1965				w.e. 15.8.1970				w.e. 14.8.1971			
	M-F		Sat		M-F		Sat		M-F		Sat		M-F		Sat		M-F		Sat		M-F		Sat	
	J	A	J	A	J	A	J	A	J	A	J	A	J	A	J	A	J	A	J	A	J	A	J	A
DOWN TRAINS																								
Maiden Newton	89		87		41		39		41		47		111		153		61		134		72		137	
Toller	15	6	14	10	5	4	10	1	9	5	4	8	16	5	19	12	9	5	7	4	7	5	5	7
Powerstock	7	4	12	8	4	4	2	3	9	3	12	8	8	5	11	6	7	3	5	5	12	1	17	5
Bridport		101		95		42		47		51		47		125		165		69		137		85		147
	111	111	113	113	50	50	51	51	59	59	63	63	135	135	183	183	77	77	146	146	91	91	159	159
UP TRAINS																								
Bridport	95		96		44		44		51		65		147		99		73		94		85		112	
Powerstock	9	10	6	11	4	3	3	1	2	7	8	8	16	9	15	5	2	5	1	6	3	13	10	16
Toller	9	12	13	15	2	5	2	7	5	5	4	26	22	15	17	11	3	7	4	7	7	8	6	5
Maiden Newton		91		89		42		41		46		43		161		115		66		86		74		107
	113	113	115	115	50	50	49	49	58	58	77	77	185	185	131	131	78	78	99	99	95	95	128	128
ALL TRAINS																								
Maiden Newton	89	91	87	89	41	42	39	41	41	46	47	43	111	161	153	115	61	66	134	86	72	74	137	107
Toller	24	18	27	25	7	9	12	8	14	10	8	34	38	20	36	23	12	12	11	11	14	13	11	12
Powerstock	16	14	18	19	8	7	5	4	11	10	20	16	24	14	26	11	9	8	6	11	15	14	27	21
Bridport	95	101	96	95	44	42	44	47	51	51	65	47	147	125	99	165	73	69	94	137	85	85	112	147
TOTAL	224	224	228	228	100	100	100	100	117	117	140	140	320	320	314	314	155	155	245	245	186	186	287	287

SOUTHERN REGION BRANCH LINES COMMITTEE.

BRANCH LINES INVESTIGATION.

BRIDPORT BRANCH.

1. LOCATION, ETC.

From the DORCHESTER - YEOVIL line at MAIDEN NEWTON to BRIDPORT, with a freight only extension to WEST BAY.

MILEAGE.

11 miles 21 chains. Single track throughout.

P.W. Classification is "D".

STATIONS.

TOLLER
POWERSTOCK
BRIDPORT
WEST BAY (Freight only).

2. ANNUAL TRAFFIC RECEIPTS. (Based on year 1950)

	Local to Branch.		Through Forwarded		Through Received		Total	
	Journeys	£	Journeys	£	Journeys	£	Journeys	£
Passengers (including Season Tickets).	51817	1830	35487	13378	49009	40909	133313	56117
			No. of Tickets.				No. of Tickets.	
Holiday Runabout Tickets.			91	64			91	64
	No.		No.		No.		No.	
Parcels	53	5	14219	4312	46892	14108	61164	18425
Milk	7							7
Livestock					111			111
Total Passenger Train Traffic.		1842		17865		55017		74724
	Tons		Tons		Tons		Tons	
Merchandise & Minerals (Ex.Cl.1-6)	30	15	2702	12673	16119	54743	18851	67431
Merchandise & Minerals (Cl.1-6)			8136	17409	3084	4971	11220	22380
Coal,Coke & Patent Fuel.			27	22	17862	29500	17889	29522
Livestock				52		859		911
Total Freight Train Traffic.		15		30156		90073		120244
Miscellaneous		861						861
GRAND TOTAL		2718		48021		145090		195829

- 2 -

3. ANNUAL ESTIMATED SAVINGS ON COMPLETE CLOSURE OF BRANCH.

		£	£
CIVIL ENGINEER			
Wages and materials		4,432	
Repairs and renewal of bridges, etc.		3,513	
Renewal of Permanent Way		2,620	10,565
SIGNAL & TELECOMMUNICATIONS ENGINEER.			
Wages and materials		255	
Renewals		381	636
TRAIN WORKING, INCLUDING GUARDS.			
Rolling Stock			
Repairs		5,563	
Renewals		363	
Wages		6,620	
Fuel,etc.		6,469	19,015
STATION ETC.EXPENSES.			
Operating Department		6,906	
Commercial Department		10,156	17,062
INTEREST SAVINGS.			
Civil Engineer		11,162	
Signal & Telecommunications Engineer		632	
Rolling Stock,etc.		1,472	13,266
			60,544

4. OTHER ITEMS OF IMPORTANCE.

Continuing liability if branch were closed for fencing,disinfestation etc. until land could be sold (included in item 3) ... ...   £2,275 per annum.

Heavy items of repairs and renewals due in next 10 years if line kept open -

Permanent Way £32,255 Bridport		
Engine Shed (1953)	3,000	£35,255

5. CONCLUSIONS AND RECOMMENDATION.

On the agreed contributive basis the line is economically sound, and it is therefore RECOMMENDED that it be retained. It is suggested, however, that Departmental consideration should be given to recovery of apparently redundant sidings at POWERSTOCK.

R.J.Hill
Operating Department (Western Region).

Chairman
Commercial Department.

G.George
Civil Engineer's Department.

Southern Region Branch Lines Committee,
EP/BL.66.
May, 1954.

fight during a period of dramatic retrenchment in the County's railways which had seen main lines such as the Somerset & Dorset, cross country lines such as the Brockenhurst – Wimborne and West Moors – Salisbury, and branch lines such as the Lyme Regis and the Swanage routes all pass into history (although the latter was of course to be dramatically reborn).

Although the Minister had supposedly ordered that the track should remain in situ for 3 years after closure, dismantling of the branch began with indecent haste on November 18 1975 using shunter 08 636, outstationed at Maiden Newton for working the recovery train which consisted of a brake van and winch, bogie and roller wagons. Loaded and empty wagons for the rails were worked by Class 52s (Westerns) to and from Westbury, re-usable concrete sleepers were taken by road to Yeovil Junction thence by rail to South Wales. Although today Bridport has an hourly bus service along the main A35 to Dorchester where intending rail passengers can join trains to Weymouth, Yeovil and Bristol, minibuses, currently operated by South West Coaches, leave Maiden Newton for Powerstock, Toller and Bridport just three times a day taking between 45 – 52 minutes to cover the route of the former railway line. Powerstock is served by an additional school trip from Bridport in the afternoon and Toller has the benefit of an additional journey from Maiden Newton to Yeovil in the early evening. Such is progress!

Posters again - this time seen during the last days of operational life of the line in April 1975. (John A. M. Vaughan courtesy RailPhotoPrints)

No passengers, but a canine customer (?) waits patiently on the platform at Toller in September 1971. (John A. M. Vaughan courtesy RailPhotoPrints)

Top - W55032 arrives at Toller while forming a Maiden Newton - Bridport service in September 1971. (John A. M. Vaughan courtesy RailPhotoPrints)

Bottom - W55032 again, this time forming a working in the reverse direction in December 1972. (John A. M. Vaughan courtesy RailPhotoPrints)

Opposite top - Devoid of track Toller awaits its fate which fortunately for the wooden building turned out to be purchase six years after closure, for £5000, dismantling and re-erection at Totnes on the DVR in 1988.

Opposite bottom - Rattling along near Toller with a Bridport service the single car provided good views of the pleasant Dorset countryside through which the branch passed. (John A. M. Vaughan courtesy RailPhotoPrints)

This page top - Unit W55032 arrives at Powerstock while forming a Maiden Newton - Bridport service in September 1971. (John A. M. Vaughan courtesy RailPhotoPrints)

This page bottom - Powerstock looking towards Bridport in 1974. The building subsequently became a B&B establishment and a book was published in 1996 detailing the struggle to buy and convert the station under the title "Powerstock Station – All Change".

Top - Powerstock seen looking towards Maiden Newton on 2 May 1975. (Derek Fear)

Left - Bradpole Crossing now devoid of signal arms and with the former crossing keeper's hut on the right deserted seen on 2 May 1975. (Derek Fear)

55032 approaches the hand operated crossing at Bradpole as it heads out of
Bridport with a Bridport - Maiden Newton service in September 1971. Latterly
the gates were operated by the train guard. Replica gates have been
constructed here by local joiners John Gale and Bernie Joy to act as a
memorial to the branch. (John A. M. Vaughan courtesy RailPhotoPrints)

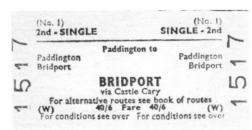

SPOTLIGHT

In each volume we will focus upon one particularly interesting location.

For this Dorset volume we feature the station at **BRIDPORT.**

Early days of dieselisation at Bridport as witnessed by the remaining steam infrastructure in the form of water crane and fire devil. The signalbox still controlled the platform starter and associated pointwork in the station area, not being closed until 8th. June 1965 after which just a single line of a "basic railway" served the platform. Diesels were introduced to the branch in 1959 so this view of a green liveried example must date from the period 1959 – 1965. (M Boddy)

Top - The single unit waits departure time at Bridport in April 1975. The station was not as convenient for the town as the old East Street station on the former extension to West Bay and by this late date was showing signs of neglect in the fabric of the building which was subsequently demolished in 1977. It was apparently last painted, green and cream, 18 years previously in 1957. Note the signboard indicating this was "Bridport for West Bay".

Right - I made my own final journey on the line during the penultimate weekend and this is the view of the terminus with a reasonable quota of passengers having alighted.

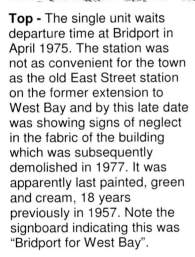

On the final day of the Bridport Branch service, 5th. May 1975, passengers await one of the last services to Maiden Newton. (John A. M. Vaughan courtesy RailPhotoPrints)

Top - W55031 stands at Bridport while forming the branch service to Maiden Newton in April 1975. (John A. M. Vaughan courtesy RailPhotoPrints)

Left - W55033 arrives at Bridport with a service from Maiden Newton in April 1975. Note the ornate lamp standard on the platform. (John A. M. Vaughan courtesy RailPhotoPrints)

Top - Buffer stop view as W55032 stands at Bridport after arrival from Maiden Newton in September 1972. This buffer stop was lifted in November 1975 signalling the start of track recovery on the branch. (John A. M. Vaughan courtesy RailPhotoPrints)

Left - With the formation of the erstwhile line to West Bay in the foreground a lone unit, so typical of branch motive power in the final years, awaits custom at Bridport.

Now unnecessarily fenced off from the platform the station building at Bridport East Street did duty as a dwelling for a number of years after passenger closure. Track was removed from this section in 1965 although the level crossing gates are still in situ in the background in this view taken in the late 1960s. The trackbed now forms part of the Bridport relief road.

Top - The dereliction of a windswept West Bay station reflects the failure of this spot to become a significant tourist resort in the railway age. Closed to passengers as a wartime measure between 31st December 1915 and 7th. July 1919, final closure came as early as September 1930.

Middle and bottom - After many years as the office of a boat yard, restoration of the station began in 1994 and track was laid and coaches arrived the following year. A Visitor Centre was established in 2001. By 2003 the two coaches had been removed since when the site has been used for cafes/restaurants by a variety of operators. In 2005 another two carriages were brought to West Bay by the 'Station Diner' operator for use as dining cars. After the failure of the business they were removed in August 2008. The station is now used as a tea shop trading as The 'Tea Station'. (M Boddy)

Top - The station seen during the construction of a car park. This was taken over in September 2012 by the production company responsible for filming the ITV television drama "Broadchurch". (M Boddy)

Right - Early on buses creamed off most of the Bridport – West Bay traffic, a tradition continued by this Bristol SUL4A single decker BDV 425C on service 405 for Western National seen in South Street Bridport in 1975. After passing through several hands subsequently, including a spell on the island of Guernsey, the vehicle was scrapped in 1986.

A summer idyll at Lyme Regis. June 1959 saw Adams radial tank 30583 with a good head of steam escaping from the safety valves at the head of an Axminster service. The engine shed glimpsed in the background together with the barley twist lamp standard and leather window strap on the inside of the open carriage door all add to the period charm. 1959 and 1960 were to be the last years when these tanks held a monopoly on branch workings, 1961 seeing the introduction of Ivatt tanks to the line. (David Smith)

Right - With vegetation growing in profusion on the platforms and trackbed, Lyme Regis station is seen some years after closure. The station building was eventually rescued in 1979 and re-erected at Alresford on the Mid Hants Railway. In the 1980s the rest of the station area was redeveloped as a small industrial estate removing all traces of the railway.

Bottom - The Achilles heel of the branch was the viaduct at Cannington which experienced subsidence problems whilst it was being built. This necessitated the provision of a "jack arch" which can be clearly seen supporting the third arch from the left and which unfortunately destroyed the symmetry of the structure.

Right - Close up of the concrete jack arch which did the job for which it was intended no further problems with the viaduct being reported during the life of the branch.

Bottom - View along the top of the viaduct looking towards Uplyme.

Opposite page - The rusting rails of the former Lyme Regis bay platform at Axminster can be seen in this view of the LCGB "A2 Commemorative Railtour" of 14th. August 1966 hauled by A2 Pacific 60532 "Blue Peter". The former branch crossed the mainline via the overbridge which can be seen in the distance.

LYME REGIS BRANCH

WEEKDAYS These timings WILL NOT APPLY ON SATURDAYS, 20th June to 12th September, 1959

Mileage M	Mileage C	DOWN		am	am	Run as Mixed Train when required	PM	PM	Commences 14th Sept.	PM Until 11th Sept. inclusive	PM	Commences 14th Sept.	PM Until 11th Sept. inclusive	PM	Commences 14th Sept.	PM Until 11th Sept. inclusive Through coach from Waterloo	PM	PM	PM
0	0	AXMINSTER dep	1	8 43	10 37		12 33	1 38		1 48	2 38		2 48	4 36		4 43	5 40	6 45	8 55
4	21	Combpyne	2	8 56	10 50		12 46	1 51		2 1	2 51		3 1	4 49		4 56	5 53	6 58	9 8
6	59	LYME REGIS arr	3	9 3½	10 57½		12 53½	1 58½		2 8½	2 58½		3 8½	4 56½		5 3½	6 0½	7 5½	9 15½

Mileage M	Mileage C	UP		am Mixed	am	am	Through coach for Waterloo until 11th Sept. inc.	PM	PM	Commences 14th Sept.	PM Until 11th Sept. inclusive	PM	PM	PM		PM
0	0	LYME REGIS dep	1	8 11	10 0	11 37		1 10	2 6		2 16	3 53	5 10	6 7	..	8 22
2	38	Combpyne	2	8 19½	10 8½	11 45½		1 18½	2 14½		2 24½	4 1½	5 18½	6 15½		8 30½
6	59	AXMINSTER arr	3	8 32	10 21	11 58		1 31	2 27		2 37	4 14	5 31	6 28	..	8 43

Left - 30583 runs round its train at Lyme Regis preparatory to returning to the junction at Axminster. These tanks were synonymous with the branch for 47 years until 1961.

Bottom - 30583 again, this time captured in the bay platform at Axminster, with the two coach 19:23 branch service on 26th. June 1960. (Dave Cobbe courtesy RailPhotoPrints)

Top - 30583 departs Combpyne with the 13:14 service to Lyme Regis on 26th. June 1960. Note the sleepers propped against the bank in readiness for some trackwork and the camping coach seen in the left background. The first camping coach was installed here in 1947 to be replaced in 1954 by an ex LSWR bogie non-corridor composite numbered S38S, 1963 being the final season during which it appeared.

Bottom - Ivatt 2-6-2T 41291 stands at Axminster with the LCGB 'East Devon Railtour' of the 7th. March 1965. These tanks, which had taken over from the Adams radials, were themselves supplanted by DMUs in November 1963. (Dave Cobbe courtesy RailPhotoPrints)

Top - An October 1958 view of the terminus with the traditional Adams tank in residence hauling coaching set No. 101. (Dave Cobbe collection courtesy RailPhotoPrints)

This page bottom, and opposite top -The end of the line for the radial tanks – Eastleigh in the winter of 1961. Two of the trio were scrapped 30584, the worst of the bunch being withdrawn in January 1961, seen left and 30582, top right, withdrawn in July 1961.This latter locomotive had run over 2 million miles in service – a remarkable achievement. (Geoff Plumb Collection)

This page bottom -
Radial survivor in the form of No. 488, erstwhile BR No. 30583, seen resplendent in LSWR livery at Sheffield Park on the Bluebell Railway. It was the only one of the trio to retain its original Adams boiler but it is attention to this component which has put the locomotive out of action since 1990 as it will probably require a completely new boiler barrel.

The Salisbury – Bournemouth line received coverage in both Volumes 1 and 3 of this series but further shots have come to light including this one of Breamore during tracklifting operations in 1965. A crane is lifting rails onto a wagon on the up line whilst trucks wait on the down line to receive recovered sleepers. (David Wigley)

(S) SOUTHERN RAILWAY. (787)

FROM WATERLOO TO

DAGGON'S ROAD

The trackbed at Daggons Road is in the process of being converted into a garden with a greenhouse, pond and steps where trains once ran. Notice the old concrete nameboard propped up on the platform.

Top - Daggons Road seen in 1967 now sports a greenhouse on the former trackbed together with geese in attendance. (Peter Russell)

Bottom - A Crompton and wagons seen at a siding near the Ferndown Industrial Estate situated between West Moors and Wimborne. The Priest's House Museum in Wimborne has a recording made in 1995 (or thereabouts) of an interview with Ted Henbest, the last stationmaster at Wimborne, who was responsible for the line up to Ringwood after closure to passengers, referring to a siding put in at the Ferndown Industrial Estate to handle ash and clinker from railway locomotive depots which was then used by a manufacturer of breeze blocks. He remarked that the traffic didn't last long as the railway was no longer able to supply the raw materials once steam had gone! Admittedly, the piles in the background don't look like the right colour for clinker, but I suspect that we at least have an explanation of what this siding was originally for. The train was picking up wagons as far as I remember. We set back into the siding from points at the Wimborne end, so the remainder of the train, including the brake van, was sitting on the old up line. The date would be either summer 1968 or just possibly 1969. (Mike Couchman)

Top - The War Department oil depot sidings at West Moors lasted in operation until 14th. October 1974. (Mike Couchman)

Middle and bottom - Two views taken on 13th. August 1976 of the oil depot sidings. The middle picture shows the former connecting line to the reception sidings and the bottom illustrates one of the sidings complete with typical MOD concrete buffer stop. (Peter Russell)

Top - West Moors seen from the guards van of a freight train returning to Poole. The crossing gates were still operated by the wheel in the signalbox until 1970. (Mike Couchman)

Bottom - On 10th April 1974 Crompton 33105 is seen returning from the military fuel depot just beyond the station. The return load of one wagon was typical of these last few months. The train had worked up from Poole to Wimborne with a 16T mineral wagon, two opens and a loaded conflat, plus brakevan. The brakevan, the 16T wagon and one open wagon had been dropped off at Wimborne on the outward run. Although the recorded closure date is the 14th October 1974, when the line beyond Wimborne was officially taken out of use, traffic to the depot had petered out at some point in the early summer with the final freight train running on 31 May 1974, with the 'Wessex Wanderer' special running the next day. The photographer's records state that goods trains ran for about another fortnight, with 'erratic' running in the second week of that period. Lifting of the BR tracks started in week commencing 14th October 1974, with lifting trains running to just west of West Moors gates. (Colin Divall)

Top - West Moors seen in the long hot summer of 1976 after track removal. (Peter Russell)

Middle - The gates at Oakley Crossing south of Wimborne were operated by hand as seen in this view taken from a freight service returning to Poole in 1968. Freight services continued to Wimborne until 1977. (Mike Couchman)

Bottom - A 1968 view of Wimborne's lengthy up platform a relic of more important days being far too long for the short services which used it latterly. (Mike Couchman)

Top - This is the view from the down platform showing, on the left of the picture, the railings surrounding the subway at this formerly very important station once the most important rail centre in the county. Its fortunes declined over the years until 1977 saw the end of the last remaining freight service.

Middle - Mobile Exhibition company "Trainex" had used the site at Wimborne for a number of years and this is a 1968 view of some of their stock parked in the yard. (Mike Couchman)

Bottom - Brush type 4 No. 1791, freshly outshopped from Eastleigh, crosses the River Stour bridge near Wimborne with the Royal Train on 11 July 1969. The train was stabled overnight, with the royal party on board, in the secluded Delph cutting between Wimborne and Broadstone. The photographer recalls the lack of security, by today's standards, as he freely wandered around the station site at Wimborne taking photographs of the train whilst staff cleaned the near derelict station and painted the platform edging white ! (Peter Russell)

Taken from the tall signalbox at Wimborne in 1971 a special working, the "Dorset Venturer" railtour, is pictured which comprised 4TC set No. 403 and propelling Crompton 6528. The entire station was built on a 30 chain curve, very evident in this view, which no doubt added to the operational difficulties at this location. (Mike Couchman)

By the 16th. October 1977, the date of this view, there was a scene of dereliction at Wimborne with weeds growing apace now that all traffic has finished. Most of the down yard had been lifted but the running lines were more or less still complete. (Colin Divall)

Top - LCGB's 'Hampshire Ferret' rail tour of 3rd February 1973 headed by Crompton Loco 6511 with 4-TC units 404 and 420, either side of buffet car 1758. The train had stopped at Wimborne in the down platform on the way back from West Moors, having worked through on the up road earlier. It is believed this was the final locomotive powered passenger train to reach West Moors, although another four were to reach Wimborne in 1976 and 1977. (Colin Divall)

Middle - Broadstone viewed from the brakevan of a freight working in 1969 which had previously visited Wimborne and was now heading for the siding shown below. (Mike Couchman)

Bottom - View looking towards Broadstone from the line to Hamworthy Junction which was singled as long ago as December 1932. The double track to Holes Bay Junction and Poole is on the right. The siding on the left was for Doulton & Co opened in June 1962 and remaining connected to Broadstone until 1973. (Mike Couchman)

Left - A rose clad Stalbridge seen in July 1967 with the rarely photographed demolition contractor's locomotive parked up with a wagonload of recovered rails. This diesel was only in use for a short time at the beginning of the main contract which involved recovery of the track from Blandford northwards to Radstock. This view is taken from the author's first S&D volume, "***Sabotaged & Defeated – Last Rites on the Somerset & Dorset***", published in 2006 and currently out of print.

Bottom - As the signalman walks back to his box Standard Class 5 73068 gets away from Sturminster Newton with a 3 coach service to Bournemouth. This 4-6-0, built in 1954, came to the S&D in May 1964 and after a brief spell of 3 months at Gloucester Horton Road in early 1965 was withdrawn from Bath Green Park shed in December 1965 to be scrapped at Cashmore's Newport the following year. (Alan Sainty Collection)

Right - Contrast the view on the previous page with this image of Sturminster Newton in July 1967 following track removal. Remarkably the station sign lies abandoned on the platform, unfortunately too large for the photographer to liberate at the time ! The dip in the platform for crossing to the opposite platform is very evident here. This picture is also taken from the author's first S&D volume.

Bottom - A happier scene at Shillingstone where the preservationists have done remarkable work in recapturing the spirit of the old station.

Opposite top - 77014 at the head of one of the post closure specials to visit the freight only stump of the S&D from Broadstone to Blandford. This was the LCGB "Dorset & Hants Railtour" of 16th. October 1966. At the rear was 76026. The tour had previously visited Ringwood and Wimborne and went on to visit Hamworthy Goods. The tour train was returned to London with 34019 and 34023 as motive power.

Opposite bottom - Following closure to freight in January 1969 track was recovered and this was the scene of desolation to be seen at Blandford in 1972 by which time the tall signalbox which had previously stood on the down platform had been demolished. (Martin Boddy)

This page top - Holes Bay junction with the former line to Broadstone going off to the right as a Standard Class 5 accelerates away with a train for Weymouth in 1967 the final year of steam on the LSWR mainline. (Peter Russell)

This page bottom - Bailey Gate signalbox photographed in April 1968 during its period of demotion to a ground frame controlling access to the adjacent creamery sidings. By the summer of that year milk traffic was spasmodic and by the following January all trains had ceased to run, the box being demolished in 1970. This view is also taken from the author's initial S&D volume.

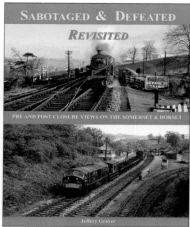

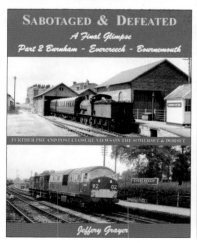

Other titles by Jeffery Grayer include:

These are certainly not 'then and now' books, but instead a selection of carefully chosen images depicting the railway in its very last months, weeks and even days of life. The trains, the stations and the people. What makes this series so different is the way Jeffery Grayer has successfully combined the story to include colour views of the demolition as well.

The first book in the series was the yellow paperback '**SABOTAGED & DEFEATED**' published by Kingfisher in 2006 and currently unavailable.

This was followed by **SABOTAGED & DEFEATED** *Revisited*
The first of the hardback series on the theme of the final days of the Somerset & Dorset.
Casebound 99.9% colour. 136 pages and also currently unavailable.
ISBN 978-1-906419-44-8   273mm x 215mm

In 2011 a new two-volume set was published with even more new material, none duplicating that already seen in the earlier volumes.

SABOTAGED & DEFEATED *A Final Glimpse:*
Part 1 Bath to Evercreech

128 pages ISBN 978-906419-90-5   £22.50
273mm x 215mm

SABOTAGED & DEFEATED *A Final Glimpse:*
Part 2 Evercreech - Burnham - Bournemouth

128 pages ISBN 978-906419-91-2   £22.50
273mm x 215mm

A signed and numbered limited edition set of Parts 1 and 2 of the two 'A Final Glimpse' volumes contained within a specially produced gold-blocked slip case is available direct from NOODLE BOOKS at £55.00.